Knitters of all skill levels will love the great designs inside. They're all knit using the Knook®, a specialized crochet hook with a cord that keeps stitches secure.

LEISURE ARTS, INC. • Maumelle, Arkansas

Dog Sweater

EASY

SHOPPING LIST

Yarn (Bulky Weight) 5

[3 ounces, 125 yards

(85 grams, 114 meters) per skein]:

- ☐ {1-1-2}{2-3-3} skein(s)

Knook

- ☐ Size L (8 mm)

  or size needed for gauge

Additional Supplies

- ☐ Yarn needle
- ☐ Sewing needle and matching thread
- ☐ 1" (25 mm) button

SIZE INFORMATION

Size	Actual Chest Measurement
X-Small	12" (30.5 cm)
Small	16" (40.5 cm)
Medium	20" (51 cm)
Large	24" (61 cm)
X-Large	28" (71 cm)
2X-Large	32" (81.5 cm)

Size Note: Choose the size closest to the actual chest measurement of the dog, measured behind the front legs. We have printed the instructions for the sizes in different colors to make it easier for you to find:

- Size X-Small in Blue
- Size Small in Pink
- Size Medium in Green
- Size Large in Purple
- Size X-Large in Red
- Size 2X-Large in Brown

Instructions in Black apply to all sizes.

GAUGE INFORMATION

In K2, P2 ribbing,

12 sts and 13 rows = 3½" (9 cm)

TECHNIQUES USED

- YO *(Fig. 2a, page 32)*
- K2 tog *(Figs. 5a & b, page 33)*
- Slip 1 as if to **knit**, K1, PSSO *(Figs. 7a & b, page 33)*

RIBBING

Ch {22-30-42}{50-58-66}.

Foundation Row: Pick up {21-29-41}{49-57-65} sts across foundation ch: {22-30-42}{50-58-66} sts.

Work in K1, P1 ribbing for {4-4½-5}{5½-6-6½}"/{10-11.5-12.5}{14-15-16.5} cm.

BODY

Row 1 (Right side)**:** K2, (P2, K2) across.

Row 2: P2, (K2, P2) across.

Repeat Rows 1 and 2 for pattern until piece measures approximately {10-12-14}{16-18-20}"/{25.5-30.5-35.5}{40.5-45.5-51} cm from foundation ch edge, ending by working Row 2.

SHAPING

Rows 1-6: K1, slip 1 as if to **knit**, K1, PSSO, knit across to last 3 sts, K2 tog, K1: {10-18-30}{38-46-54} sts.

Bind off all sts in **knit**.

TUMMY STRAP

Ch {12-18-24}{30-36-42}.

Foundation Row: Pick up {11-17-23}{29-35-41} sts across foundation ch: {12-18-24}{30-36-42} sts.

Knit {2-2-4}{6-8-8} rows.

Buttonhole Row: K1, YO (**buttonhole made**), K2 tog, K2, YO (**buttonhole made**), K2 tog, knit across.

Knit {2-2-4}{6-8-8} rows.

Bind off all sts in **knit**.

FINISHING

Sew Tummy Strap to right edge of Body, beginning {6½-7½-8½}{9½-10½-11½}"/{16.5-19-21.5}{24-26.5-29} cm from foundation ch edge.

Weave ends of rows of K1, P1 Ribbing together ***(Fig. 13, page 35)***.

Sew button to left side of Body opposite Tummy Strap.

Design by Shelle Hendrix.

Hat

EASY

SHOPPING LIST

Yarn (Bulky Weight)

[3.5 ounces, 127 yards (100 grams, 116 meters) per skein]:

☐ {2-2-2}{3-3-3} skeins

Knook

☐ Size K (6.5 mm) **or** size needed for gauge

Additional Supplies

☐ Markers - 7

☐ Yarn needle

☐ Embellishments - button, cord, feather

SIZE INFORMATION

Size	Finished Size
Child Small	16½" (42 cm)
Child Medium	18" (45.5 cm)
Child Large	19½" (49.5 cm)
Adult Small	21" (53.5 cm)
Adult Medium	22½" (57 cm)
Adult Large	24" (61 cm)

Size Note: We have printed the instructions for the sizes in different colors to make it easier for you to find:

- Child Small in Blue
- Child Medium in Pink
- Child Large in Green
- Adult Small in Purple
- Adult Medium in Red
- Adult Large in Brown

Instructions in Black apply to all sizes.

GAUGE INFORMATION

In K1, P1 ribbing, 16 sts and 20 rnds = 4" (10 cm)

TECHNIQUE USED

- K2 tog ***(Figs. 5a & b, page 33)***

BRIM

Ch {60-66-72}{78-84-90}.

Foundation Rnd: Bring first ch around to meet last ch made, being careful **not** to twist ch, pick up a st in first {59-65-71}{77-83-89} chs, place a marker to indicate the beginning of the rnd ***(see Markers and Circular Knitting, page 31)***: {60-66-72}{78-84-90} sts.

Work in K1, P1 ribbing until piece measures approximately {7-8-9}{10-11-12}"/{18-20.5-23}{25.5-28-30.5} cm from foundation ch edge.

TOP SHAPING

Rnd 1: K{8-9-10}{11-12-13}, K2 tog, ★ place marker, K{8-9-10}{11-12-13}, K2 tog; repeat from ★ around: {54-60-66}{72-78-84} sts.

Rnd 2: Knit around.

Rnd 3 (Decrease rnd): ★ Knit around to within 2 sts of next marker, K2 tog, slip marker; repeat from ★ around: {48-54-60}{66-72-78} sts.

Repeat Rnds 2 and 3, {6-7-8}{9-10-11} times: 12 sts.

Cut yarn leaving a long end. Thread yarn needle with end and weave through sts on cord; remove cord and weave end through sts once **more**. Pull tightly to close; secure end.

Turn Brim up and embellish Hat as desired.

Lacy Leg Warmers

EASY

SHOPPING LIST

Yarn (Medium Weight)

[3.5 ounces, 170 yards (100 grams, 156 meters) per skein]:

☐ 1{1-2} skein(s)

Knook

☐ Size I (5.5 mm) **or** size needed for gauge

Additional Supply

☐ Marker

SIZE INFORMATION

Size	Finished Length & Calf Circumference
Small	12" x 8" (30.5 cm x 20.5 cm)
Medium	12½" x 10" (32 cm x 25.5 cm)
Large	13" x 12" (33 cm x 30.5 cm)

Size Note: We have printed the instructions for the sizes in different colors to make it easier for you to find:

- Size Small in Blue
- Size Medium in Pink
- Size Large in Green

Instructions in Black apply to all sizes.

GAUGE INFORMATION

In Stockinette Stitch (knit every round), 16 sts and 22 rnds = 4" (10 cm)

TECHNIQUES USED

- YO ***(Fig. 2a, page 32)***
- K2 tog ***(Figs. 5a & b, page 33)***
- Slip 1 as if to **knit**, K1, PSSO ***(Figs. 7a & b, page 33)***
- Slip 1 as if to **knit**, K2 tog, PSSO ***(Fig. 8, page 33)***

LEG WARMER (Make 2)

Ch 32{40-48}.

Foundation Rnd: Bring first ch around to meet last ch made and being careful **not** to twist ch, pick up a st in first 31{39-47} chs, place a marker to indicate the beginning of the rnd ***(see Markers and Circular Knitting, page 31)***: 32{40-48} sts.

Rnds 1-6: (K1, P1) around.

Rnd 7: Knit around.

Rnd 8: ★ YO, slip 1 as if to **knit**, K2 tog, PSSO, YO, K5; repeat from ★ around.

Rnds 9-11: Repeat Rnds 7 and 8 once, then repeat Rnd 7 once **more**.

Rnd 12: ★ K3, YO, slip 1 as if to **knit**, K1, PSSO, K1, K2 tog, YO; repeat from ★ around.

Rnd 13: Knit around.

Rnd 14: ★ YO, slip 1 as if to **knit**, K2 tog, PSSO, YO, K1; repeat from ★ around.

Rnds 15-43: Repeat Rnds 7-14, 3 times; then repeat Rnds 7-11 once **more**.

Rnd 44: ★ YO, slip 1 as if to **knit**, K2 tog, PSSO, YO, slip 1 as if to **knit**, K1, PSSO, K1, K2 tog; repeat from ★ around: 24{30-36} sts.

Rnd 45: Knit around.

Rnd 46: ★ YO, slip 1 as if to **knit**, K2 tog, PSSO, YO, K3; repeat from ★ around.

Repeat Rnds 45 and 46 until Leg Warmer measures approximately 10{10½-11}"/25.5{26.5-28} cm from foundation ch edge **or** 2" (5 cm) less than desired finished length.

Work in K1, P1 ribbing for 2" (5 cm).

Bind off all sts **loosely** in pattern.

Design by Cynthia Guggemos.

Quick Scarf

EASY

Finished Size: 7" x 81" (18 cm x 205.5 cm)

SHOPPING LIST

Yarn (Bulky Weight) BULKY 5

[5 ounces, 153 yards

(140 grams, 140 meters) per skein**]**:

- ☐ 2 skeins

Knook

- ☐ Size L (8 mm)

  or size needed for gauge

GAUGE INFORMATION

In Stockinette Stitch

(knit one row, purl one row),

8 sts and 10 rows = 3" (7.5 cm)

TECHNIQUES USED

- YO ***(Figs. 2a & b, page 32)***
- K2 tog ***(Figs. 5a & b, page 33)***
- Slip 1 as if to **knit**, K1, PSSO ***(Figs. 7a & b, page 33)***
- Slip 1, K2 tog, PSSO ***(Fig. 8, page 33)***

When instructed to slip a stitch, always slip it as if to **knit**.

SCARF

Ch 21.

Foundation Row: Pick up 20 sts across foundation ch: 21 sts.

Row 1: Knit across.

Row 2 (Right side)**:** Slip 1, K1, K2 tog, YO, K2, YO, slip 1, K1, PSSO, K2 tog, YO, K1, YO, slip 1, K1, PSSO, K2 tog, YO, K2, K2 tog, YO, K2.

Row 3 AND ALL WRONG SIDE ROWS: Slip 1, K1, K2 tog, YO, P 13, K2 tog, YO, K2.

Row 4: Slip 1, K1, K2 tog, YO, K2, YO, slip 1, K1, PSSO, K2 tog, YO, K1, YO, slip 1, K1, PSSO, K2 tog, YO, K2, K2 tog, YO, K2.

Row 6: Slip 1, K1, K2 tog, YO, K3, YO, slip 1, K1, PSSO, K3, K2 tog, YO, K3, K2 tog, YO, K2.

Row 8: Slip 1, K1, K2 tog, YO, K4, YO, slip 1, K1, PSSO, K1, K2 tog, YO, K4, K2 tog, YO, K2.

Row 10: Slip 1, K1, K2 tog, YO, K5, YO, slip 1, K2 tog, PSSO, YO, K5, K2 tog, YO, K2.

Row 12: Slip 1, K1, K2 tog, YO, K4, K2 tog, YO, K1, YO, slip 1, K1, PSSO, K4, K2 tog, YO, K2.

Row 14: Slip 1, K1, K2 tog, YO, K3, K2 tog, YO, K3, YO, slip 1, K1, PSSO, K3, K2 tog, YO, K2.

Row 16: Slip 1, K1, K2 tog, YO, K2, K2 tog, YO, K5, YO, slip 1, K1, PSSO, K2, K2 tog, YO, K2.

Row 18: Slip 1, K1, K2 tog, YO, K2, YO, slip 1, K1, PSSO, K2 tog, YO, K1, YO, slip 1, K1, PSSO, K2 tog, YO, K2, K2 tog, YO, K2.

Row 20: Slip 1, K1, K2 tog, YO, K2, YO, slip 1, K1, PSSO, K2 tog, YO, K1, YO, slip 1, K1, PSSO, K2 tog, YO, K2, K2 tog, YO, K2.

Repeat Rows 5-20 for pattern until Scarf measures approximately 80" (203 cm) from foundation ch edge, ending by working Row 20.

Last Row: Knit across.

Bind off all sts in **knit**.

Design by Kay Meadors.

A Spot For Pets

EASY

SHOPPING LIST

Yarn (Super Bulky Weight) SUPER BULKY 6

[5 ounces, 81 yards

(142 grams, 74 meters) per skein]:

- ☐ Tan - 6 skeins
- ☐ Red - 6 skeins

Knook

- ☐ Size M (9 mm)

or size needed for gauge

Additional Supplies

- ☐ Markers - 2
- ☐ Batting
- ☐ Yarn needle

SIZE INFORMATION

Size	Finished Measurement
Small	23" (58.5 cm) square
Medium	29" (73.5 cm) square
Large	34½" (87.5 cm) square

Size Note: We have printed the instructions for the sizes in different colors to make it easier for you to find:

- Size Small in Blue
- Size Medium in Pink
- Size Large in Green

Instructions in Black apply to all sizes.

GAUGE INFORMATION

In Stockinette Stitch

(knit one row, purl one row).

10 sts and 14 rows = 4" (10 cm)

FRONT

With Tan, ch 58{72-86} sts.

Foundation Row: Pick up 57{71-85} sts across foundation ch: 58{72-86} sts.

Work in Stockinette Stitch (knit one row, purl one row) until Front measures approximately 2¾{5¾-8½}"/7{14.5-21.5} cm from foundation ch edge, ending by working a **purl** row.

Next Row: K7{14-21}, place marker ***(see Markers, page 31)***, K 16, drop Tan ***(Fig. 11, page 34)***, with Red, K 12, with second Tan, K 16, place marker, K7{14-21}.

Next 60 Rows: Work even following chart between markers.

With Tan, work in Stockinette Stitch for approximately 2¾{5¾-8½}"/ 7{14.5-21.5} cm, ending by working a **purl** row.

Bind off all sts in **knit**.

BACK

Work same as Front, reversing colors.

FINISHING

Sew Front and Back together, inserting desired layers of batting before closing. If desired, tack batting to bed at center and corners, sewing through all layers to secure.

Design by Peggy Schultz.

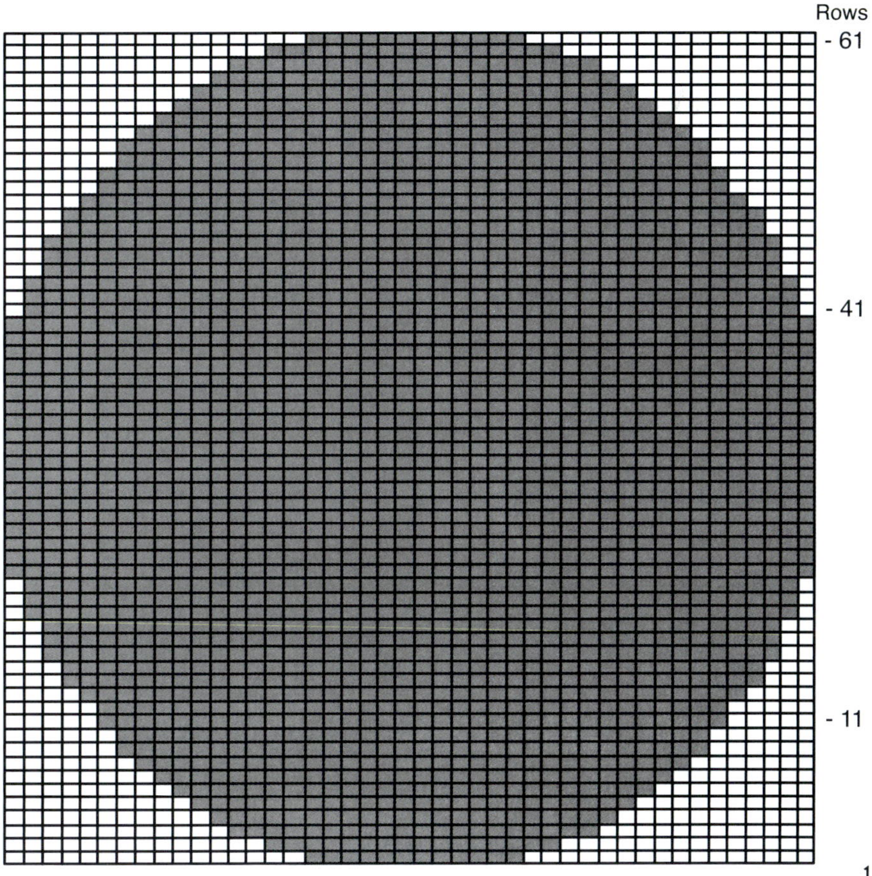

Slipper Socks

EASY

SHOPPING LIST

Yarn (Medium Weight) 4

[7 ounces, 364 yards
(198 grams, 333 meters) per skein]:

☐ 1 skein

Knook

☐ Size I (5.5 mm)
or size needed for gauge

Additional Supplies

☐ Split-ring marker

☐ Yarn needle

SIZE INFORMATION

Size	Finished Length & Circumference
Child	10" x 5¼" (25.5 cm x 13.5 cm)
Pre-teen	11¼" x 6½" (28.5 cm x 16.5 cm)
Adult Small	13" x 7¾" (33 cm x 19.5 cm)
Adult Large	15½" x 9" (39.5 cm x 23 cm)

Size Note: We have printed the instructions for the sizes in different colors to make it easier for you to find:

- Size Child in Blue
- Size Pre-teen in Pink
- Size Adult Small in Green
- Size Adult Large in Purple

Instructions in Black apply to all sizes.

GAUGE INFORMATION

In Stockinette Stitch
(knit each round),
16 sts and 22 rnds = 4" (10 cm)
In Spiral Pattern,
16 sts and 26 rows/rnds = 4" (10 cm)

Gauge Swatch: 4" (10 cm) square
Ch 16.
Foundation Row: Pick up 15 sts across foundation ch: 16 sts.
Row 1: (K3, P2) 3 times, K1.
Row 2: P2, K2, (P3, K2) twice, P2.
Row 3: K1, (P2, K3) across.
Row 4: K1, (P3, K2) across.
Row 5: P1, (K3, P2) across.
Row 6: P1, (K2, P3) across.
Row 7: K2, P2, (K3, P2) twice, K2.
Row 8: (P3, K2) 3 times, P1.
Row 9: (P2, K3) 3 times, P1.
Row 10: (K2, P3) 3 times, K1.
Rows 11-26: Repeat Rows 1-10 once, then repeat Rows 1-6 once **more**.
Bind off all sts.

TECHNIQUE USED

- K2 tog ***(Figs. 5a & b, page 33)***

SOCK (Make 2)

LEG

Ch 21{26-31-36}.

Foundation Rnd: Bring first ch around to meet last ch made and being careful **not** to twist ch, pick up a st in first 20{25-30-35} chs ***(see Circular Knitting, page 31)***: 21{26-31-36} sts.

Because the number of stitches is one more than a complete pattern repeat, a continuous spiral will form as you work. It is not necessary to mark the beginning of a round or to keep track of which round you are on throughout the Leg.

★ K3, P2; repeat from ★ working in continuous rounds until Leg measures approximately 9{10-11½-13½}"/23{25.5-29-34.5} cm from foundation ch edge.

TOE

Place marker around the first stitch to indicate the beginning of the round ***(see Markers, page 31)***.

ADULT LARGE SIZE ONLY

Rnd 1: (K7, K2 tog) 4 times: 32 sts.

Rnd 2: Knit around.

Rnd 3: (K6, K2 tog) 4 times: 28 sts.

Rnd 4: Knit around.

Rnd 5: (K5, K2 tog) 4 times: 24 sts.

Rnd 6: Knit around.

Rnd 7: (K4, K2 tog) 4 times: 20 sts.

Rnd 8: Knit around.

Rnd 9: (K3, K2 tog) 4 times: 16 sts.

Rnd 10: Knit around.

Rnd 11: K2 tog around: 8 sts.

ADULT MEDIUM SIZE ONLY

Rnd 1: K 13, K2 tog, (K6, K2 tog) twice: 28 sts.

Rnds 2-9: Work same as Adult Large Rnds 4-11: 8 sts.

PRE-TEEN SIZE ONLY

Rnd 1: K 17, K2 tog, K5, K2 tog: 24 sts.

Rnds 2-7: Work same as Adult Large Rnds 6-11: 8 sts.

CHILD SIZE ONLY

Rnd 1: K 19, K2 tog: 20 sts.

Rnds 2-5: Work same as Adult Large Rnds 8-11: 8 sts.

ALL SIZES

Cut yarn leaving an 8" (20.5 cm) end for sewing. Thread yarn needle with end and slip remaining sts from cord onto yarn needle; gather tightly to close and secure end.

Design by Cynthia Guggemos.

Lattice Tunic

INTERMEDIATE

SHOPPING LIST

Yarn (Medium Weight) 4

[6 ounces, 315 yards

(170.1 grams, 288 meters) per skein]:

- ☐ 3{4-4-4} skeins

Knook

- ☐ Size H (5 mm)

or size needed for gauge

Additional Supplies

- ☐ Extra cords - 2
- ☐ Yarn needle

SIZE INFORMATION

Size	Finished Chest Measurement
X-Small	30½" (77.5 cm)
Small	34¼" (87 cm)
Medium	38" (96.5 cm)
Large	42" (106.5 cm)

Size Note: We have printed the instructions for the sizes in different colors to make it easier for you to find:

- Size X-Small in Blue
- Size Small in Pink
- Size Medium in Green
- Size Large in Purple

Instructions in Black apply to all sizes.

GAUGE INFORMATION

In Body pattern,

17 sts and 25 rows = 4" (10 cm)

TECHNIQUES USED

- M1 ***(Figs. 3a & b, page 32)***
- M1P ***(Figs. 4a & b, page 32)***
- K2 tog ***(Figs. 5a & b, page 33)***
- Slip 1 as if to **knit**, K1, PSSO ***(Figs. 7a & b, page 33)***

When instructed to slip a stitch, always slip as if to **purl** with the yarn in **back** unless otherwise instructed.

BACK

BORDER

Ch 66{74-82-90}.

Foundation Row: Pick up 65{73-81-89} sts across foundation ch: 66{74-82-90} sts.

Row 1: Knit across.

Row 2 (Right side)**:** Knit across.

Row 3: P1, (K1, slip 1) across to last st, P1.

Row 4: Knit across.

Row 5: P1, (slip 1, K1) across to last st, P1.

Repeat Rows 2-5 for pattern until Border measures approximately 2½" (6.5 cm) from foundation ch edge, ending by working a **wrong** side row.

BODY

Row 1: K 33{37-41-45}, M1, knit across: 67{75-83-91} sts.

Row 2: Knit across.

Row 3: K1, P1, (K7, P1) across to last st, K1.

Row 4: P2, K1, P5, K1, (P1, K1, P5, K1) across to last 2 sts, P2.

Row 5: K3, (P1, K3) across.

Row 6: P4, K1, P1, K1, (P5, K1, P1, K1) across to last 4 sts, P4.

Row 7: K5, P1, (K7, P1) across to last 5 sts, K5.

Row 8: P4, K1, P1, K1, (P5, K1, P1, K1) across to last 4 sts, P4.

Row 9: K3, (P1, K3) across.

Row 10: P2, K1, P5, K1, (P1, K1, P5, K1) across to last 2 sts, P2.

Repeat Rows 3-10 for pattern until Back measures approximately 13{13½-13¾-14}"/33{34.5-35-35.5} cm from foundation ch edge, ending by working a **wrong** side row.

ARMHOLE SHAPING

Maintain established pattern throughout.

Rows 1 and 2: Bind off 3{4-4-5} sts at the beginning of the next 2 rows, work across: 61{67-75-81} sts.

Row 3 (Decrease row)**:** K1, slip 1 as if to **knit**, K1, PSSO, work across to last 3 sts, K2 tog, K1: 59{65-73-79} sts.

Row 4: Work across.

Rows 5 thru 7{11-15-17}: Repeat Rows 3 and 4, 1{3-5-6} time(s); then repeat Row 3 once **more**: 55{57-61-65} sts.

Work even until Armholes measure approximately 7¾{8-8¼-8¾}"/19.5{20.5-21-22} cm, ending by working a **wrong** side row.

SHOULDER SHAPING

Rows 1 and 2: Bind off 10{10-5-6} sts at the beginning of the next 2 rows, work across: 35{37-51-53} sts.

Sizes Medium and Large Only

Rows 3 and 4: Bind off 6 sts at the beginning of the next 2 rows, work across: {39-41} sts.

All Sizes: Unthread Knook and leave remaining 35{37-39-41} sts on the cord; cut yarn.

FRONT

Work same as Back until Armholes measure approximately 5{5-5¼-5½}"/12.5{12.5-13.5-14} cm, ending by working a **right** side row: 55{57-61-65} sts.

At the end of the last row, turn; pull cord out the row below, unthread Knook and leave stitches on cord. Thread Knook with extra cord to work Dividing Row.

Dividing Row: Work across 17{17-18-20} sts, pull Knook through sts, unthread the extra cord from the Knook, pull first cord out of the row below sts just worked and thread Knook with end of first cord, bind off next 21{23-25-25} sts, work across: 17{17-18-20} sts on **each** cord.

NECK SHAPING - FIRST SIDE

Row 1 (Decrease row)**:** Work across to within 3 sts of Neck edge, slip 1 as if to **knit**, K1, PSSO, K1: 16{16-17-19} sts.

Row 2: Work across.

Rows 3 thru 13{13-13-15}: Repeat Rows 1 and 2, 5{5-5-6} times; then repeat Row 1 once **more**: 10{10-11-12} sts.

Work even until First Side measures same as Back to Shoulder Shaping, ending by working a **wrong** side row.

SHOULDER SHAPING

Sizes X-Small and Small Only

Bind off remaining sts; cut yarn.

Sizes Medium and Large Only

Row 1: Bind off {5-6} sts, work across.

Row 2: Bind off remaining sts; cut yarn.

NECK SHAPING - SECOND SIDE

With **right** side facing, thread Knook with the neck edge end of the remaining cord.

Row 1 (Decrease row)**:** K1, K2 tog, work across: 16{16-17-19} sts.

Row 2: Work across.

Rows 3 thru 13{13-13-15}: Repeat Rows 1 and 2, 5{5-5-6} times; then repeat Row 1 once **more**: 10{10-11-12} sts.

Work even until Second Side measures same as Back to Shoulder Shaping, ending by working a **right** side row.

SHOULDER SHAPING

Complete same as First Side.

SLEEVE (Make 2)

BORDER

Ch 50{50-58-58}.

Foundation Row: Pick up 49{49-57-57} sts across foundation ch: 50{50-58-58} sts.

Row 1: Knit across.

Row 2 (Right side)**:** Knit across.

Row 3: P1, (K1, slip 1) across to last st, P1.

Row 4: Knit across.

Row 5: P1, (slip 1, K1) across to last st, P1.

Repeat Rows 2-5 for pattern until Border measures approximately 2½" (6.5 cm) from foundation ch edge, ending by working a **wrong** side row.

BODY

Row 1: K 25{25-29-29}, M1, knit across: 51{51-59-59} sts.

Row 2: Knit across.

Row 3: K1, P1, (K7, P1) across to last st, K1.

Row 4: P2, K1, P5, K1, (P1, K1, P5, K1) across to last 2 sts, P2.

Row 5: K3, (P1, K3) across.

Row 6: P4, K1, P1, K1, (P5, K1, P1, K1) across to last 4 sts, P4.

Row 7: K5, P1, (K7, P1) across to last 5 sts, K5.

Row 8: P4, K1, P1, K1, (P5, K1, P1, K1) across to last 4 sts, P4.

Row 9: K3, (P1, K3) across.

Row 10: P2, K1, P5, K1, (P1, K1, P5, K1) across to last 2 sts, P2.

Sizes X-Small and Medium Only

Repeat Rows 3-10 for pattern until Sleeve measures approximately 11{11½}"/28{29} cm from foundation ch edge, ending by working a **wrong** side row.

Sizes Small and Large Only

Rows 11-23: Repeat Rows 3-10 once, then repeat Rows 3-7 once **more**.

Row 24: P1, M1P, P3, K1, P1, K1, (P5, K1, P1, K1) across to last 4 sts, P3, M1P, P1: {53-61} sts.

Row 25: K4, P1, (K3, P1) across to last 4 sts, K4.

Row 26: P3, K1, P5, K1, (P1, K1, P5, K1) across to last 3 sts, P3.

Row 27: K2, P1, (K7, P1) across to last 2 sts, K2.

Row 28: P3, K1, P5, K1, (P1, K1, P5, K1) across to last 3 sts, P3.

Row 29: K4, P1, (K3, P1) across to last 4 sts, K4.

Row 30: P5, (K1, P1, K1, P5) across.

Row 31: K6, P1, (K7, P1) across to last 6 sts, K6.

Row 32: P5, (K1, P1, K1, P5) across.

Rows 33-47: Repeat Rows 25-32 once, then repeat Rows 25-31 once **more**.

Row 48: P1, M1P, P4, K1, P1, K1, (P5, K1, P1, K1) across to last 5 sts, P4, M1P, P1: {55-63} sts.

Row 49: K5, P1, (K3, P1) across to last 5 sts, K5.

Row 50: P4, K1, P5, K1, (P1, K1, P5, K1) across to last 4 sts, P4.

Row 51: K3, P1, (K7, P1) across to last 3 sts, K3.

Row 52: P4, K1, P5, K1, (P1, K1, P5, K1) across to last 4 sts, P4.

Row 53: K5, P1, (K3, P1) across to last 5 sts, K5.

Row 54: P6, K1, P1, K1, (P5, K1, P1, K1) across to last 6 sts, P6.

Row 55: K7, (P1, K7) across.

Row 56: P6, K1, P1, K1, (P5, K1, P1, K1) across to last 6 sts, P6.

Repeat Rows 49-56 for pattern until Sleeve measures approximately {11¼-11¾}"/{28.5-30} cm from foundation ch edge, ending by working a **wrong** side row.

SLEEVE CAP - ALL SIZES

Maintain established pattern throughout.

Rows 1 and 2: Bind off 3{4-4-5} sts at the beginning of the next 2 rows, work across: 45{47-51-53} sts.

Row 3 (Decrease row)**:** K1, slip 1 as if to **knit**, K1, PSSO, work across to last 3 sts, K2 tog, K1: 43{45-49-51} sts.

Row 4: Work across.

Continue to decrease one stitch in same manner at each edge every other row, 14{15-16-15} times **more**; then decrease every row, 0{0-0-2} times ***(see Zeros, page 31)***: 15{15-17-17} sts.

Bind off all sts.

FINISHING

Sew shoulder seams.

NECKBAND

Rnd 1: With **right** side facing, thread Knook with cord from Back, join yarn and K 35{37-39-41} sts; pick up 14{15-16-17} sts evenly spaced across Front Neck edge ***(Figs. 12a & b, page 35)***, pick up 21{23-25-25} sts along bound off edge of Front, pick up 14{15-16-17} sts evenly spaced across Front Neck edge, place a marker to indicate the beginning of the rnd ***(see Markers, page 31)***: 84{90-96-100} sts.

Rnd 2: Purl around.

Rnd 3: Knit around.

Rnd 4: (P1, with yarn in **front**, slip 1) around.

Rnd 5: Knit around.

Rnd 6: (With yarn in **front**, slip 1, P1) around.

Rnd 7: Knit around.

Bind off all sts **loosely** in **knit**.

Set in Sleeves, placing center of Sleeve Cap at shoulder seam and matching Armhole bind off.

Beginning at top of Border on Body, weave underarm and side in one continuous seam ***(Fig. 13, page 35)***.

Design by Cynthia Guggemos.

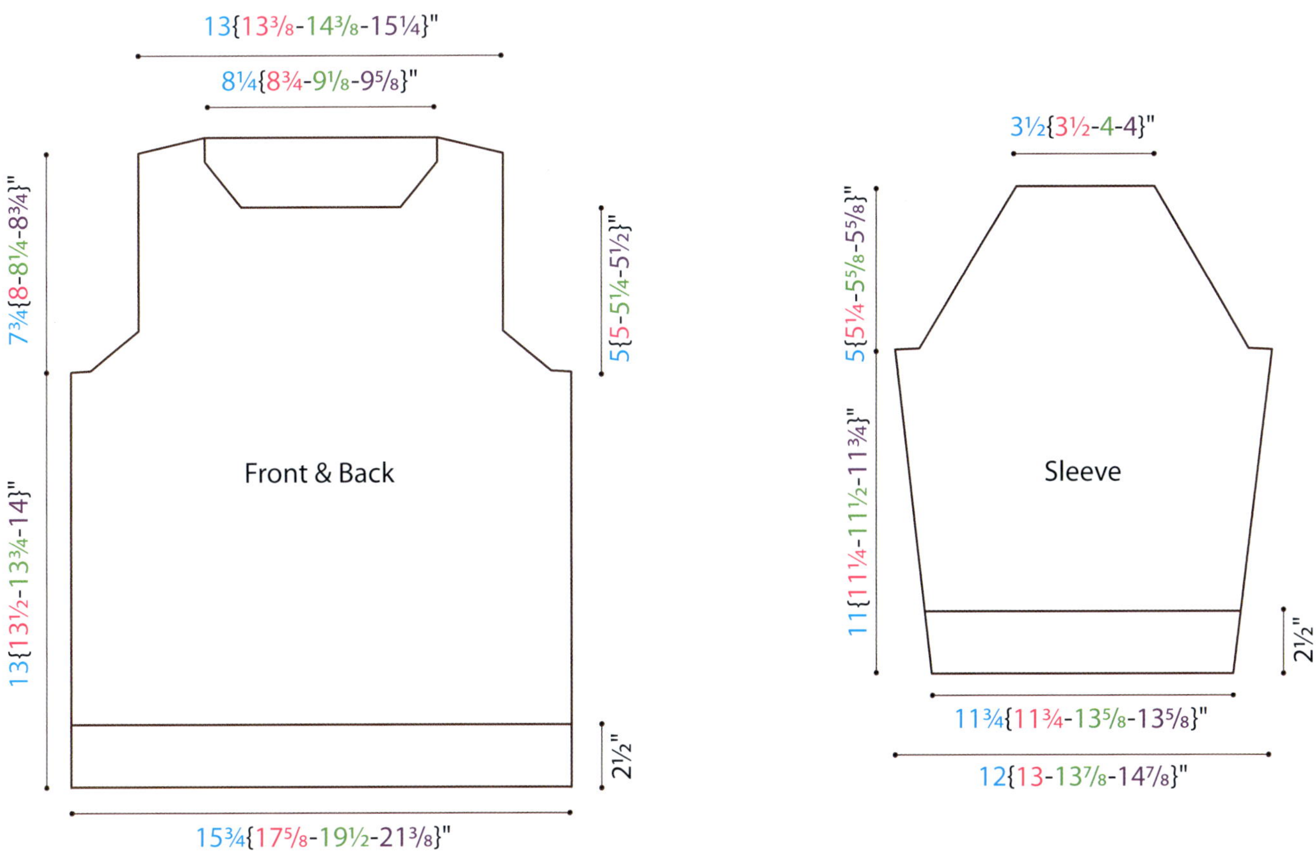

Note: Pieces include 2 edge stitches.

Eyelet Shrug

EASY

SHOPPING LIST

Yarn (Fine Weight) 2

[3.5 ounces, 317 yards (100 grams, 290 meters) per skein]:

- ☐ 2 skeins

Knook

- ☐ Size H (5 mm) **or** size needed for gauge

Additional Supplies

- ☐ Cable needle
- ☐ Yarn needle

SIZE INFORMATION

Size	Chest Measurement
X-Small	28-30" (71-76 cm)
Small	32-34" (81.5-86.5 cm)
Medium	36-38" (91.5-96.5 cm)
Large	40-42" (101.5-106.5 cm)
X-Large	44-46" (112-117 cm)

Size Note: We have printed the instructions for the sizes in different colors to make it easier for you to find:

- X-Small in Blue
- Small in Pink
- Medium in Green
- Large in Purple
- X-Large in Red

Instructions in Black apply to all sizes.

GAUGE INFORMATION

In Stockinette Stitch (knit one row, purl one row), 20 sts and 26 rows = 4" (10 cm)

TECHNIQUES USED

- YO ***(Fig. 2a, page 32)***
- K2 tog ***(Figs. 5a & b, page 33)***
- K2 tog tbl ***(Fig. 6, page 33)***
- Slip 1 as if to **knit**, K1, PSSO ***(Figs. 7a & b, page 33)***

When instructed to slip a stitch, always slip it as if to **knit**.

FIRST HALF

Ch {67-67}{77-77-87}.

Foundation Row: Pick up {66-66}{76-76-86} sts across foundation ch: {67-67}{77-77-87} sts.

Row 1: Purl across.

Row 2 (Right side)**:** K6, K2 tog, YO, K1, YO, slip 1, K1, PSSO, ★ K5, K2 tog, YO, K1, YO, slip 1, K1, PSSO; repeat from ★ across to last 6 sts, K6.

Rows 3 thru {67-67}{79-79-91}: Repeat Rows 1 and 2, {32-32}{38-38-44} times; then repeat Row 1 once **more**.

Decrease Row: Slip 1, K1, PSSO, K4, K2 tog, YO, K1, YO, slip 1, K1, PSSO, ★ K5, K2 tog, YO, K1, YO, slip 1, K1, PSSO; repeat from ★ across to last 6 sts, K4, K2 tog: {65-65}{75-75-85} sts.

Maintaining pattern, continue to decrease one stitch at **each** edge in same manner every 12 rows, 4 times: {57-57}{67-67-77} sts.

Work even until First Half measures {21½-22½}{23-23½-25}"/{54.5-57}{58.5-59.5-63.5} cm from foundation ch edge **or** 3" (7.5 cm) less than desired length of sleeve, ending by working Row 1.

EDGING

Row 1: K1, ★ K2 tog, YO, K1, YO, slip 1, K1, PSSO; repeat from ★ across to last st, K1.

Row 2: Purl across.

Repeat Rows 1 and 2 until Edging measures 3" (7.5 cm), ending by working Row 2.

Last Row: K1, K2 tog, YO, K1, YO, slip 1, K1, PSSO, ★ YO, K2 tog, YO, K1, YO, slip 1, K1, PSSO; repeat from ★ across to last st, K1: {67-67}{79-79-91} sts.

Bind off all sts as follows: K2, slip sts just knit from Knook onto cable needle ***(Fig. A)***, insert Knook through back loops of both sts on cable needle ***(Fig. B)***, K2 tog tbl, ★ knit next st on cord, slip 2 sts from Knook onto cable needle and K2 tog tbl; repeat from ★ across; finish off leaving a long end for sewing.

Fig. A

Fig. B

SECOND HALF

Work same as First Half.

FINISHING

With **right** sides of both pieces together, sew foundation ch edges together.

With **right** side together, sew each sleeve seam {16½-16½}{17-17-17½}"/{42-42}{43-43-44.5} cm from bound off edge of Edging.

Design by Kay Meadors.

Spa Set

EASY

SHOPPING LIST

Yarn (Medium Weight) MEDIUM 4

[2.5 ounces, 120 yards
(70.9 grams, 109 meters) per skein]:

- ☐ 3 skeins

Knooks

- ☐ Size E (3.5 mm) **and**
- ☐ Size G (4 mm)
  or sizes needed for gauge

Additional Supplies

- ☐ Markers
- ☐ Extra cord
- ☐ Yarn needle
- ☐ ¼" (7 mm) wide ribbon - 18" (45.5 cm) length

FINISHED SIZE INFORMATION

Headband: 19" (48.5 cm) circumference
Bath Mitt: Adult
Soap Sack: 7" circumference x 6½" high (18 cm x 16.5 cm)
Facecloth: 8¼" wide x 8¾" high (21 cm x 22 cm)

GAUGE INFORMATION

With larger size Knook,
in Stockinette Stitch
(knit one row, purl one row),
17 sts and 26 rows = 4" (10 cm)

TECHNIQUES USED

- YO ***(Fig. 2a, page 32)***
- M1 ***(Figs. 3a & b, page 32)***
- K2 tog ***(Figs. 5a & b, page 33)***
- Slip 1 as if to **knit**, K1, PSSO ***(Figs. 7a & b, page 33)***
- Slip 1 as if to **knit**, K2 tog, PSSO ***(Fig. 8, page 33)***
- P2 tog ***(Fig. 9, page 34)***

HEADBAND

With larger size Knook and leaving a long end for sewing, ch 83.

Foundation Row: Pick up 82 sts across foundation ch: 83 sts.

Row 1 (Right side)**:** Knit across.

Row 2: K4, P3, (K5, P3) across to last 4 sts, K4.

Row 3: P4, K3, (P5, K3) across to last 4 sts, P4.

Row 4: K4, P3, (K5, P3) across to last 4 sts, K4.

Row 5: Knit across.

Row 6: P3, (K5, P3) across.

Row 7: K3, (P5, K3) across.

Row 8: P3, (K5, P3) across.

Rows 9-16: Repeat Rows 1-8.

Bind off all sts in **knit**.

Sew ends of rows together.

BATH MITT

RIBBING

With smaller size Knook, ch 39.

Foundation Row: Pick up 38 sts across foundation ch: 39 sts.

Row 1: P1, (K1, P1) across.

Row 2: K1, (P1, K1) across.

Rows 3-12: Repeat Rows 1 and 2, 5 times.

BODY

Change to larger size Knook.

Row 1 (Right side)**:** Knit across.

Row 2 AND ALL EVEN NUMBERED ROWS THROUGH Row 22: Purl across.

Row 3: K3, YO, slip 1 as if to **knit**, K1, PSSO, ★ K6, YO, slip 1 as if to **knit**, K1, PSSO; repeat from ★ across to last 2 sts, K2.

Row 5: K2, YO, slip 1 as if to **knit**, K2 tog, PSSO, ★ YO, K5, YO, slip 1 as if to **knit**, K2 tog, PSSO; repeat from ★ across to last 2 sts, YO, K2.

Row 7: K3, YO, slip 1 as if to **knit**, K1, PSSO, ★ K6, YO, slip 1 as if to **knit**, K1, PSSO; repeat from ★ across to last 2 sts, K2.

Row 9: K 19, place marker *(see Markers, page 31)*, M1, K1, M1, place marker, knit across: 41 sts.

Row 11: K7, YO, slip 1 as if to **knit**, K1, PSSO, K6, YO, slip 1 as if to **knit**, K1, PSSO, K2, slip next marker, M1, K3, M1, slip next marker, K3, (YO, slip 1 as if to **knit**, K1, PSSO, K6) twice: 43 sts.

Row 13: K6, YO, slip 1 as if to **knit**, K2 tog, PSSO, YO, K5, YO, slip 1 as if to **knit**, K2 tog, PSSO, YO, K2, slip next marker, M1, K5, M1, slip next marker, K2, YO, slip 1 as if to **knit**, K2 tog, PSSO, YO, K5, YO, slip 1 as if to **knit**, K2 tog, PSSO, YO, K6: 45 sts.

Row 15: K7, YO, slip 1 as if to **knit**, K1, PSSO, K6, YO, slip 1 as if to **knit**, K1, PSSO, K2, slip next marker, M1, K7, M1, slip next marker, K3, (YO, slip 1 as if to **knit**, K1, PSSO, K6) twice: 47 sts.

Row 17: Knit across to next marker, slip marker, M1, K9, M1, slip next marker, knit across: 49 sts.

Row 19: K3, (YO, slip 1 if as to **knit**, K1, PSSO, K6) twice, slip next marker, M1, K 11, M1, slip next marker, K7, YO, slip 1 as if to **knit**, K1, PSSO, K6, YO, slip 1 as if to **knit**, K1, PSSO, K2: 51 sts.

Row 21: K2, YO, slip 1 as if to **knit**, K2 tog, PSSO, YO, K5, YO, slip 1 as if to **knit**, K2 tog, PSSO, YO, K6, slip next marker, M1, K 13, M1, slip next marker, K6, YO, slip 1 as if to **knit**, K2 tog, PSSO, YO, K5, YO, slip 1 as if to **knit**, K2 tog, PSSO, YO, K2: 53 sts.

Row 23: K3, (YO, slip 1 as to **knit**, K1, PSSO, K6) twice, remove next marker, thread yarn needle with extra cord and slip next 15 sts onto extra cord for thumb, remove next marker; skipping sts on extra cord, K7, YO, slip 1 as if to **knit**, K1, PSSO, K6, YO, slip 1 as if to **knit**, K1, PSSO, K2: 38 sts.

Row 24: Purl across.

Row 25: Knit across.

Rows 26-37: Repeat Rows 24 and 25, 6 times.

Row 38: P 19, place marker, P 19.

Row 39 (Decrease row)**:** Slip 1 as if to **knit**, K1, PSSO, knit across to within 2 sts of marker, K2 tog, slip marker, slip 1 as if to **knit**, K1, PSSO, knit across to last 2 sts, K2 tog: 34 sts.

Row 40: Purl across.

Rows 41-48: Repeat Rows 39 and 40, 4 times: 18 sts.

Row 49: K2 tog across: 9 sts.

Row 50: Purl across.

Cut yarn leaving a 12" (30.5 cm) end for sewing. Thread yarn needle with end and slip remaining sts from cord onto yarn needle; gather tightly to close; secure end but do **not** cut yarn.

THUMB

Row 1: With **right** side facing, thread larger size Knook with end of extra cord, knit across skipped sts: 15 sts.

Row 2: P6, P2 tog, P7: 14 sts.

Row 3: Knit across.

Row 4: Purl across.

Rows 5-10: Repeat Rows 3 and 4, 3 times.

Row 11: K2 tog across: 7 sts.

Cut yarn leaving an 8" (20.5 cm) end for sewing. Thread yarn needle with end and slip remaining sts from cord onto yarn needle; gather tightly to close; secure end and sew Thumb seam.

With remaining end, sew side seam.

SOAP SACK

With larger size Knook, ch 62.

Foundation Row: Pick up 61 sts across foundation ch: 62 sts.

Row 1 (Right side)**:** Knit across.

Row 2: Purl.

Rows 3-6: Repeat Rows 1 and 2 twice.

Row 7: K2 tog across: 31 sts.

Row 8: Purl across.

Row 9: Knit across.

Row 10: Purl across.

Row 11 (Eyelet row)**:** K1, (YO, K2 tog) across.

Rows 12-17: Repeat Rows 8 and 9, 3 times.

Row 18 AND ALL EVEN-NUMBERED ROWS THROUGH Row 30: Purl across.

Row 19: K3, YO, slip 1 as if to **knit**, K1, PSSO, ★ K6, YO, slip 1 as if to **knit**, K1, PSSO; repeat from ★ across to last 2 sts, K2.

Row 21: K2, YO, slip 1 as if to **knit**, K2 tog, PSSO, ★ YO, K5, YO, slip 1 as if to **knit**, K2 tog, PSSO; repeat from ★ across to last 2 sts, YO, K2.

Row 23: K3, YO, slip 1 as if to **knit**, K1, PSSO, ★ K6, YO, slip 1 as if to **knit**, K1, PSSO; repeat from ★ across to last 2 sts, K2.

Row 25: Knit across.

Row 27: K7, (YO, slip 1 as if to **knit**, K1, PSSO, K6) across.

Row 29: K6, YO, slip 1 as if to **knit**, K2 tog, PSSO, (YO, K5, YO, slip 1 as if to **knit**, K2 tog, PSSO) twice, YO, K6.

Row 31: K7, (YO, slip 1 as if to **knit**, K1, PSSO, K6) across.

Rows 32-40: Repeat Rows 8 and 9, 4 times; then repeat Row 8 once **more**.

Row 41: K1, K2 tog across: 16 sts.

Cut yarn leaving a 10" (25.5 cm) end for sewing. Thread yarn needle with end and slip remaining sts from cord onto yarn needle; gather tightly to close; secure end and sew seam.

Weave ribbon through Eyelet row.

FACECLOTH

With larger size Knook, ch 37.

Foundation Row: Pick up 36 sts across foundation ch: 37 sts.

Rows 1-4: K1, (P1, K1) across.

Row 5 (Right side)**:** K1, P1, K 33, P1, K1.

Row 6 AND ALL EVEN-NUMBERED ROWS: K1, P1, K1, P 31, K1, P1, K1.

Row 7: K1, P1, K4, YO, slip 1 as if to **knit**, K1, PSSO, ★ K6, YO, slip 1 as if to **knit**, K1, PSSO; repeat from ★ across to last 5 sts, K3, P1, K1.

Row 9: K1, P1, K3, YO, slip 1 as if to **knit**, K2 tog, PSSO, ★ YO, K5, YO, slip 1 as if to **knit**, K2 tog, PSSO; repeat from ★ across to last 5 sts, YO, K3, P1, K1.

Row 11: K1, P1, K4, YO, slip 1 as if to **knit**, K1, PSSO, ★ K6, YO, slip 1 as if to **knit**, K1, PSSO; repeat from ★ across to last 5 sts, K3, P1, K1.

Row 13: K1, P1, K 33, P1, K1.

Row 15: K1, P1, K8, YO, slip 1 as if to **knit**, K1, PSSO, (K6, YO, slip 1 as if to **knit**, K1, PSSO) twice, K7, P1, K1.

Row 17: K1, P1, K7, YO, slip 1 as if to **knit**, K2 tog, PSSO, (YO, K5, YO, slip 1 as if to **knit**, K2 tog, PSSO) twice, YO, K7, P1, K1.

Row 19: K1, P1, K8, YO, slip 1 as if to **knit**, K1, PSSO, (K6, YO, slip 1 as if to **knit**, K1, PSSO) twice, K7, P1, K1.

Row 21: K1, P1, K 33, P1, K1.

Rows 22-52: Repeat Rows 6-21 once, then repeat Rows 6-20 once **more**.

Rows 53-56: K1, (P1, K1) across.

Bind off all sts in **knit**.

Designs by Rhonda White.

Purse

EASY

Finished Size: 10" wide x 10" high (25.5 cm x 25.5 cm) (excluding Straps)

Shown on page 29.

SHOPPING LIST

Yarn (Bulky Weight) BULKY 5

[5 ounces, 153 yards
(140 grams, 140 meters) per skein]:

☐ 2 skeins

Knook

☐ Size K (6.5 mm)
or size needed for gauge

Additional Supplies

☐ Split-ring markers - 4
☐ Extra cord
☐ 1¾" (4.5 cm) rings - 8
☐ Fabric for lining - ½ yard (½ meter)
☐ ½" (12 mm) covered poly boning - ⅝ yard (.57 meters)
☐ Magnetic clasp
☐ Sewing needle and thread
☐ Yarn needle

GAUGE INFORMATION

In pattern,
14 sts and 18 rows = 4" (10 cm)

TECHNIQUES USED

- K2 tog ***(Figs. 5a & b, page 33)***
- P2 tog tbl ***(Fig. 10, page 34)***

STITCH GUIDE

KNIT AND PURL INCREASE

Knit the next stitch, then bring the yarn under the Knook to the **front** of the work and purl into the **front** loop of the same stitch ***(Fig. A)***.

PURL AND KNIT INCREASE

Purl the next stitch, then bring the yarn under the Knook to the **back** of the work and knit into the **back** loop of the same stitch ***(Fig. B)***.

Fig. A

Fig. B

BODY (Make 2)

Ch 24.

Foundation Row: Pick up 23 sts across foundation ch: 24 sts.

Row 1: (K1, P1) across.

Row 2 (Right side)**:** Work knit and purl increase twice, (K1, P1) across: 26 sts.

Rows 3 and 4: Work purl and knit increase twice, (P1, K1) across: 30 sts.

Rows 5 and 6: Work knit and purl increase twice, (K1, P1) across: 34 sts.

Row 7: Work purl and knit increase twice, (P1, K1) across: 36 sts.

Row 8: (P1, K1) across.

Rows 9 and 10: (K1, P1) across.

Rows 11 and 12: (P1, K1) across.

Repeat Rows 9-12 for pattern until Body measures approximately 8¾" (22 cm) from foundation ch edge, ending by working Row 12.

Place a marker in first and last st on last row.

At the end of the last row, turn; unthread Knook and leave sts on cord. Thread Knook with second cord to work Dividing Row.

Dividing Row: P2 tog tbl, K1, (P1, K1) 6 times, pull Knook through sts, leaving sts just worked on second cord. Unthread the Knook, pull end of first cord out of the row below sts on second cord. Thread Knook with first cord, bind off next 8 sts in pattern, (K1, P1) across to last 2 sts, K2 tog: 14 sts on second cord and 12 sts on first cord.

TOP SHAPING

FIRST SIDE

Row 1: (P1, K1) across.

Row 2: Bind off 2 sts, P1, (K1, P1) across to last 2 sts, K2 tog: 9 sts.

Row 3: P1, (K1, P1) across.

Row 4: Bind off 2 sts, (K1, P1) twice, K2 tog: 6 sts.

Row 5: (P1, K1) across.

STRAP

Row 1: Do **not** turn; bring working yarn **behind** sts, K6.

Repeat Row 1 until Strap measures approximately 27" (68.5 cm).

Bind off all sts in **knit**.

SECOND SIDE

Row 1: With **right** side facing, thread Knook with end of second cord closest to First Side, bind off 2 sts, K1, (P1, K1) across: 12 sts.

Row 2: P2 tog tbl, (K1, P1) across: 11 sts.

Row 3: Bind off 2 sts, (P1, K1) across: 9 sts.

Row 4: P2 tog tbl, K1, (P1, K1) across: 8 sts.

Row 5: Bind off 2 sts, K1, (P1, K1) twice: 6 sts.

Bind off all sts in **purl**.

Weave Strap through first set of rings as follows: Come up through first ring, down through second ring **and** first ring, then up through second ring ***(Photo A)***. Slide rings to beginning end of Strap.

Photo A

Weave Strap through second set of rings as follows: Go down through first ring, up through second ring **and** first ring, then down through second ring ***(Photo B)***.

Photo B

Sew end of Strap to 6 bound off sts on Top Shaping. Slide second set of rings over seam.

FINISHING

Using Body as a pattern, cut 2 pieces of fabric ¼" (7 mm) larger than Body, beginning and ending at markers; then cut lining straight across the top, ½" (12 mm) above markers.

With **wrong** sides of Body together and beginning at one marker, sew pieces together, ending at next marker.

Matching right sides and using a ½" (12 mm) seam allowance, sew lining along long curved edge. Clip curved edge. Press 1" (2.5 cm) to wrong side along top edge of lining. Cut 2 strips of boning equal to the width of the lining's top edge. Remove plastic boning from fabric sleeve. Position sleeve ¼" (7 mm) below fold line on wrong side of lining and stitch to lining, working over existing stitch lines. Stitch across one end of boning sleeve. Trim ¼" (7 mm) off plastic boning, reinsert in sleeve and stitch second end closed. Repeat for second side. Attach magnetic clasp to lining, working around plastic boning. Insert lining into purse and sew top edge of lining to purse.

Design by Joan Beebe.

General Instructions

ABBREVIATIONS

ch(s)	chain(s)
cm	centimeters
K	knit
M1	make one
M1P	make one purl
mm	millimeters
P	purl
PSSO	pass slipped stitch over
Rnd(s)	round(s)
st(s)	stitch(es)
tbl	through back loop
tog	together
YO	yarn over

SYMBOLS & TERMS

★ — work instructions following ★ as many **more** times as indicated in addition to the first time.

( ) or [ ] — work enclosed instructions **as many** times as specified by the number immediately following **or** work all enclosed instructions in the stitch or space indicated **or** contains explanatory remarks.

colon (:) — the number(s) given after a colon at the end of a row or round denotes the number of stitches you should have on that row or rnd.

work even — work without increasing or decreasing in the established pattern.

GAUGE

Gauge is the number of stitches and rows in every inch of your knitted piece. Exact gauge is **essential** for proper size. Before beginning your project, make a sample swatch in the yarn and Knook specified. After completing the swatch, measure it, counting your stitches and rows carefully. If your swatch is larger or smaller than specified, **make another, changing Knook size to get the correct gauge.** Keep trying until you find the size Knook that will give you the specified gauge.

Yarn Weight Symbol & Names	SUPER FINE 1	FINE 2	LIGHT 3	MEDIUM 4	BULKY 5	SUPER BULKY 6
Type of Yarns in Category	Sock, Fingering Baby	Sport, Baby	DK, Light Worsted	Worsted, Afghan, Aran	Chunky, Craft, Rug	Bulky, Roving
Knook Gauge Ranges in Stockinette St to 4" (10 cm)	27-32 sts	23-26 sts	21-24 sts	16-20 sts	12-15 sts	6-11 sts
Advised Knook Size Range	B-1 to D-3	D-3 to F-5	F-5 to G-6	G-6 to I-9	I-9 to K-10½	M-13 and larger

KNOOK TERMINOLOGY		
UNITED STATES		**INTERNATIONAL**
gauge	=	tension
bind off	=	cast off
yarn over (YO)	=	yarn forward (yfwd) **or** yarn around needle (yrn)

KNOOKS									
U.S.	E-4	F-5	G-6	H-8	I-9	J-10	K-10½	L-11	M-13
Metric - mm	3.5	3.75	4	5	5.5	6	6.5	8	9

BEGINNER	Projects for first-time stitchers using basic knit and purl stitches. Minimal shaping.
EASY	Projects using basic stitches, repetitive stitch patterns, simple color changes, knitting in the round techniques, and simple shaping and finishing.
INTERMEDIATE	Projects with a variety of stitches, such as basic cables and lace, simple intarsia, and mid-level shaping and finishing.
EXPERIENCED	Projects using advanced techniques and stitches, such as short rows, fair isle, more intricate intarsia, cables, lace patterns, and numerous color changes.

ZEROS

To consolidate the length of an involved pattern, zeros are sometimes used so that all sizes can be combined. For example, decrease every row, 0{0-0-2} times means that the first 3 sizes would do nothing and the largest size would decrease twice.

MARKERS

As a convenience to you, we have used markers to help distinguish the beginning of a pattern or a round. Place markers as instructed. You may use purchased markers or tie a length of contrasting color yarn around the cord. When you reach a marker on a row or round, slip it onto the Knook; remove it when no longer needed.

CIRCULAR KNITTING

When you knit a tube, as for a hat or a sock, you are going to work around and around on the outside of the circle with the **right** side of the knitting facing you.

To begin working in the round, chain the number called for in your project.

Bring the first chain around to meet the last chain made, making sure that the chain isn't twisted ***(Fig. 1a).***

Fig. 1a

Begin by picking up a stitch in the first chain ***(Fig. 1b)*** and in each chain around. Remember that the loop on the Knook counts as your first stitch.

Fig. 1b

Before beginning your first round, place a marker on the Knook before the first stitch ***(Fig. 1c)***, **or** place a split-ring marker around the first stitch to indicate the beginning of the round.

Fig. 1c

INCREASES

YARN OVER *(abbreviated YO)*

After a knit stitch and before a knit stitch:

Bring the yarn to the front **under** the Knook, then back **over** the top of the Knook so that it is now in position to **knit** the next stitch *(Fig. 2a)*.

Fig. 2a

After a knit stitch and before a purl stitch:

Bring the yarn to the front **under** the Knook, then back **over** the top of the Knook and forward **under** the Knook again so that it is now in position to **purl** the next stitch *(Fig. 2b)*.

Fig. 2b

MAKE ONE *(abbreviated M1)*

With yarn in **back**, insert the Knook under the horizontal strand between the stitches from the **back** to the **front** *(Fig. 3a)*, then knit into that strand *(Fig. 3b)*.

Fig. 3a

Fig. 3b

MAKE ONE PURL

(abbreviated M1P)

With yarn in **front**, insert the Knook under the horizontal strand between the stitches from the **front** to the **back** *(Fig. 4a)*, then purl into that strand *(Fig. 4b)*.

Fig. 4a

Fig. 4b

DECREASES

KNIT 2 TOGETHER

(abbreviated K2 tog)

Insert the Knook into the **front** of the second and then the first stitch on the cord as if to **knit** ***(Fig. 5a)***, then **knit** them together as if they were one stitch ***(Fig. 5b)***.

Fig. 5a

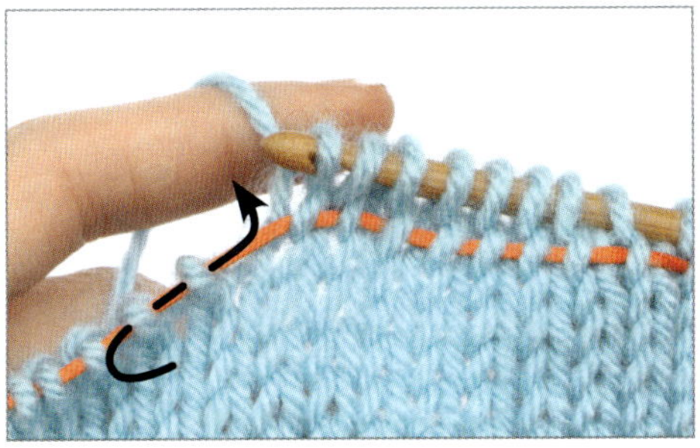

Fig. 5b

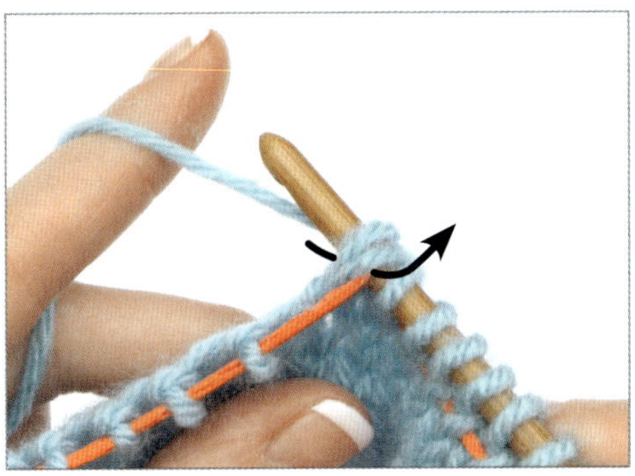

KNIT 2 TOGETHER THROUGH BACK LOOP

(abbreviated K2 tog tbl)

Insert the Knook into the **back** of the first 2 stitches on the cord ***(Fig. 6)***, then **knit** them together as if they were one stitch.

Fig. 6

SLIP 1, KNIT 1, PASS SLIPPED STITCH OVER

(abbreviated slip 1, K1, PSSO)

Slip one stitch as if to **knit** ***(Fig. 7a)***. Knit the next stitch. Pull the stitch just made through the slipped stitch ***(Fig. 7b)***.

Fig. 7a

Fig. 7b

SLIP 1, KNIT 2 TOGETHER, PASS SLIPPED STITCH OVER

(abbreviated slip 1, K2 tog, PSSO)

Slip one stitch as if to **knit** ***(Fig. 7a)***. Knit the next 2 stitches together ***(Figs. 5a & b)***. Pull the stitch just made through the slipped stitch ***(Fig. 8)***.

Fig. 8

PURL 2 TOGETHER

(abbreviated P2 tog)

Insert the Knook into the **front** of the first 2 stitches on the cord as if to **purl** ***(Fig. 9)***, then purl them together as if they were one stitch.

Fig. 9

PURL 2 TOGETHER THROUGH BACK LOOP

(abbreviated P2 tog tbl)

Insert the Knook into the **back** loop of the second stitch and the first stitch on the cord as if to **knit** ***(Fig. 10)***, then purl them together as if they were one stitch.

Fig. 10

CHANGING COLORS

When changing colors, always pick up the new color yarn from **beneath** the dropped yarn and keep the color which has just been worked to the side ***(Fig. 11)***. This will avoid holes in the finished piece. Take extra care to keep your tension even.

Fig. 11

PICKING UP STITCHES

When instructed to pick up stitches on a knitted piece, insert the Knook from the **front** to the **back** under two strands at the edge ***(Figs. 12a & b)***. Catch the yarn as if picking up stitches on the foundation chain and draw the loop through, resulting in a stitch on the Knook.

Fig. 12a

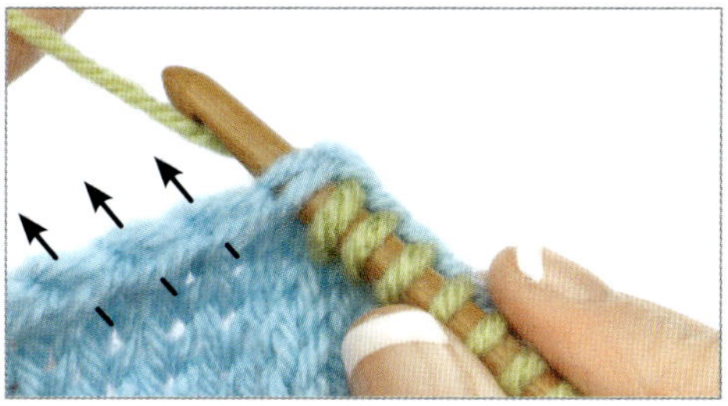

Fig. 12b

Repeat this along the edge to pick up the required amount of stitches.

WEAVING SEAMS

With **right** side of both pieces facing you and edges even, sew through both sides once to secure the beginning of the seam. Insert the needle under the bar **between** the first and second stitches on the row and pull the yarn through ***(Fig. 13)***. Insert the needle under the next bar on the second side. Repeat from side to side, being careful to match rows. If the edges are different lengths, it may be necessary to insert the needle under two bars at one edge.

Fig. 13

Yarn Information

The projects in this book were made using a variety of yarn weights. Any brand of the specified weight of yarn may be used. It is best to refer to the yardage/meters when determining how many balls or skeins to purchase. Remember, to achieve the finished size, it is the GAUGE/TENSION that is important, not the brand of yarn.

For your convenience, listed below are the specific yarns used to create our photography models. Because yarn manufacturers make frequent changes in their product lines, you may sometimes find it necessary to use a substitute yarn or to search for the discontinued product at alternate suppliers (locally or online).

DOG SWEATER
Patons® Shetland Chunky™
#67532 Deep Red Tweed

HAT
Lion's Pride® Woolspun®
#123 Taupe

LACY LEG WARMERS
Lion Brand® Vanna's Choice®
#151 Charcoal Grey

QUICK SCARF
Lion Brand® Wool-Ease® Chunky
#133 Pumpkin

A SPOT FOR PETS
Lion Brand® Hometown USA®
Tan - #099 Los Angeles Tan
Red - #189 Napa Valley Pinot

SLIPPER SOCKS
Red Heart® Super Saver®
#718 Shocking Pink

LATTICE TUNIC
Caron® Simply Soft®
#9755 Sunshine

EYELET SHRUG
Premier Yarns® Cotton Fair®
#2704 Turquoise

SPA SET
Lily® Sugar'n Cream®
#04 Ecru

PURSE
Lion Brand® Wool-Ease® Chunky
#402 Wheat

Production Team: Instructional/Technical Writer - Sarah J. Green; Editorial Writer - Susan Frantz Wiles; Senior Graphic Artist - Lora Puls; Graphic Artist - Victoria Temple; and Photographer - Ken West.

Hat made and instructions tested by Nancy Desmarais.